Also by
GARY A. ROSENBERG

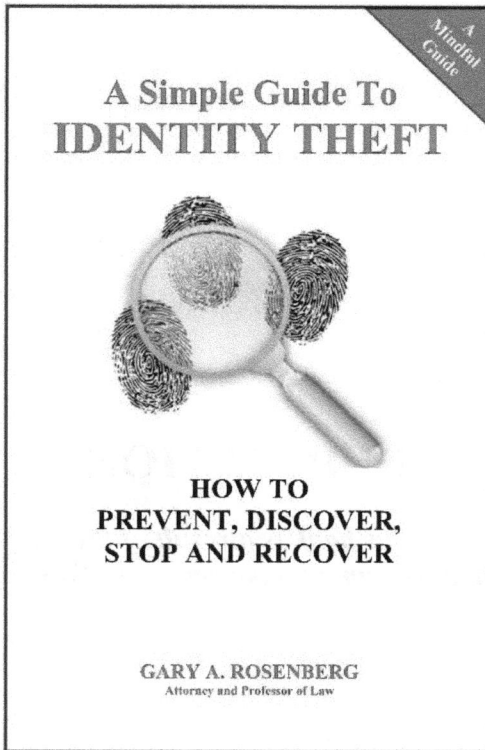

A Mindful Guide

A Simple Guide To
IDENTITY THEFT

HOW TO
PREVENT, DISCOVER,
STOP AND RECOVER

GARY A. ROSENBERG
Attorney and Professor of Law

This is the definitive book on how to prevent, discover, stop and recover from identity theft. It explains how identity theft can take place and how you can prevent it from happening. More importantly, it provides the tools for you to discover if you are already the victim of identity theft and to stop it from getting worse and then recover your good name and finances.

This book is the essential guide to protect against the growing crime of identity theft. This book is a "must-have" read!

Written by a practicing Attorney who is also a Professor of Law. The information provided includes an Action Plan as well as forms, sample letters and applicable law to guide you through the process of eliminating identity theft and its ramifications from your life.

AVAILABLE ON AMAZON

DEDICATION

This book is a result of the encouragement, inspiration and love of Shaks

About the Author

GARY A. ROSENBERG

Gary A. Rosenberg is the President of the Law Offices Of Gary A. Rosenberg, A Professional Corporation located in California. Mr. Rosenberg was admitted to the practice of law in 1978 and since has amassed a wealth of experience in personal and consumer law, cyber-bullying, family law, business and corporate law, insurance and credit law.

Mr. Rosenberg is a frequent writer and lecturer on law for national and international concerns, as well as professional organizations and public and private schools. In addition to his active law practice and writing and lecturing schedule, Mr. Rosenberg is a Professor of Law, teaching in the legal areas of Remedies, Sales and Secured Transactions and Debtor-Creditor Relations. Mr. Rosenberg also holds a Lifetime Teaching Credential in Law for the California Community Colleges.

The Law Offices Of Gary A. Rosenberg, A Professional Corporation is a full service law firm, offering sophisticated counsel and nationwide litigation management to a wide range of individual, consumer, institutional, business and governmental clients.

Mr. Rosenberg obtained his Bachelor of Arts degree from UCLA with a major in Psychology, and obtained a Juris Doctor degree from Southwestern University School of Law. Mr. Rosenberg is a member of the State Bar of California and is also admitted to practice before the United States District Courts for the Southern, Central, Eastern and Northern Districts of California, the United States Court of Appeals for the Ninth Circuit as well as the United States Tax Court. In addition to an active law practice, Mr. Rosenberg has been a member of the National Association of Retail Collection Attorneys ("NARCA"), the Commercial Law League of America ("CLLA"), and the National Association of Subrogation Professionals ("NASP").

IF YOU WOULD LIKE TO ARRANGE AN EVENT FOR YOUR SCHOOL OR ORGANIZATION WITH MR. ROSENBERG SPEAKING ON CYBERBULLYING, CONTACT THE PUBLISHER AT: info@mindfulguidepublishing.com

Copyrighted Material

ISBN-13: 978-0-692-64681-6
ISBN-10: 0692646817

Library of Congress Control Number:

Published by Mindful Guide Publishing
6400 Canoga Avenue, Suite 205, Woodland Hills, CA 91367
info@mindfulguidepublishing.com

IF YOU WOULD LIKE TO ARRANGE AN EVENT FOR YOUR SCHOOL OR ORGANIZATION WITH MR. ROSENBERG SPEAKING ON CYBERBULLYING, CONTACT THE PUBLISHER AT: info@mindfulguidepublishing.com

Table of Contents

Chapter 1: **INTRODUCTION**   Page 1

Chapter 2: **IN THE BEGINNING THERE WAS BULLYING AND HARASSMENT**   Page 5

       What is Bullying?   Page 5

       What is Harassment?   Page 7

Chapter 3: **OUR KIDS DON'T LIVE WITH US: THEY LIVE IN A CYBER WORLD**   Page 11

       A Brief History Of Our Kids' Cyber World   Page 11

       How Pervasive is Social Media?   Page 13

       How Much Time is Spent on Social Media?   Page 16

Chapter 4: **WHAT IS CYBERBULLYING?**   Page 19

       What is Cyberbullying?   Page 19

       What Makes Cyberbullying Different Than "Regular" Bullying and Harassment?   Page 20

       How is Cyberbullying Done?   Page 21

       How Prevalent is Cyberbullying?   Page 22

       Who Is At Risk Of Being Cyberbullied?   Page 25

       Who Is More Likely To Bully Others?   Page 26

Chapter 5: **THE RAMIFICATIONS OF CYBERBULLYING Understand the Problem**   Page 29

       The Effects Of Cyberbullying On The Victim   Page 29

       The Effects Of Cyberbullying On The Bully   Page 34

       The Effects Of Cyberbullying On The Bystander   Page 35

Chapter 6: **THERE'S NO PRIVACY IN THE CYBER WORLD**   Page 37

       How Private Is The Cyber World?   Page 37

       How Private Are Your Kids? What Do They Share With Others?   Page 41

Chapter 7: WARNING SIGNS OF CYBERBULLYING   Page 43

         Warning Signs That A Child Is A Victim
         Of Cyberbullying   Page 43

         Warning Signs That A Child Is Bullying   Page 45

**Chapter 8: THERE ARE FEDERAL AND STATE
PROTECTIONS AGAINST CYBERBULLYING**   Page 47

         Federal Laws   Page 47

         State Laws   Page 49

**Chapter 9: LIABILITY OF A BULLY:
It Doesn't Matter If He Or She Is A Minor!**   Page 53

Chapter 10: LIABILITY OF A PARENT OF A BULLY   Page 55

**Chapter 11: OBLIGATIONS OF A SCHOOL
AS TO CYBERBULLYING**   Page 59

         Federal Laws   Page 59

         State Laws   Page 61

**Chapter 12: WHAT'S A COMMUNITY TO DO TO
PREVENT CYBERBULLYING?**   Page 63

**Chapter 13: WHAT'S A PARENT TO DO TO
PREVENT CYBERBULLYING?**   Page 65

         Ever Feel This Frustrated With Your Child?   Page 65

         Some Suggestions On How to Prevent
         Cyberbullying   Page 66

**Appendix: SOME INTERNET ACRONYMS
EVERY PARENT SHOULD KNOW**   Page 83

Chapter 1

INTRODUCTION

I have been a practicing Attorney since 1978, and have been a Professor of Law for more than 15 years. That, however, is not why I wrote this book. The inspiration for this book in the Mindful Guide series was my own personal experience. I have three wonderful children, and their health and safety has always been of concern. Knowing that my concerns and those of my clients are shared by parents everywhere (or should be shared by parents everywhere!), it became my goal through the writing of this book to bring some of what I have learned over time to other parents in the hope it may be of some benefit.

I think it is safe to say that none of us who are parents feel any greater responsibility than we do to our children. Our greatest joy is in being parents, and our greatest fears are because we are parents.

As if we don't already have enough to worry about as parents, we now must recognize a new and ever-growing risk to the well-being of our children. The newest risk we need to understand and contend with is electronic technology in all its myriad forms.

Electronic technology has not only become a necessary part of our children's educational lives, but it has to some extent, become the principal make-up of their social world.

We all have come to recognize from friends and the news and probably from some of our own experiences that one of the fastest growing concerns parents have for their children is in the realm of the ever-growing and pervasive "Cyber World" where our children now reside.

We are already familiar with cybercrime stories, and hacking and data theft. As parents we are all concerned about our kids facing the online threats of adults posing as youth. We worry about the psychological effects on our children that online content and social media may have. We worry about our kids being too easily exposed to porn or obscene or troubling media.

Quite simply, parents need to determine what type of content and concerns they have with regard to their children's use of the internet.

> The Cyber World is electronic technology
>
> Electronic technology includes devices and equipment such as cell phones, computers, and tablets as well as communication tools including social media sites, text messages, chat and websites

This book will highlight a new reality and a new concern: the growing epidemic of harassment and bullying that is taking place throughout the Cyber World – the world of electronic technology.

Our concerns require us to understand what the problem encompasses, how pervasive it is, how one can and should monitor and deal with and prevent our children from wandering into the world of harassment and cyberbullying.

We will explore in this book what the Cyber World really means to our kids. We will see that the Cyber World opens up the real risk of our kids experiencing or causing cyberbullying. We will see the extent of the problem, and sadly, the ramifications on our children and society from this horrible epidemic. Ultimately, I hope that you will come to appreciate that there are things you can do as a parent to prevent and correct cyberbullying if it involves your children or others.

So congratulations to you in buying this book to learn more about the Cyber World in which our children live. In doing so, you will come to better know what some of the risks are to our children, why they exist, and what needs to be done. More to the point, this book is designed to help you see cyberbullying as harassment in the modern age, and ultimately, how to protect our children.

> ## CYBERBULLYING:
>
> ## UNDERSTAND IT, DEAL WITH IT AND KEEP KIDS SAFE!

Chapter 2

IN THE BEGINNING THERE WAS BULLYING AND HARASSMENT

What Is Bullying?

Before we can consider cyberbullying, we first need to recognize that the foundation and birthplace of cyberbullying is just plain old-fashioned bullying and harassment.

The United States Department of Health & Human Services defines bullying as:

> "Bullying is unwanted, aggressive behavior among school aged children that involves a real or perceived power imbalance. The behavior is repeated, or has the potential to be repeated, over time. Both kids who are bullied and who bully others may have serious, lasting problems.
>
> In order to be considered bullying, the behavior must be aggressive and include:
>
> - An Imbalance of Power: Kids who bully use their power—such as physical strength, access to embarrassing information, or popularity—to control or harm others. Power imbalances can change over time and in different situations, even if they involve the same people.
>
> - Repetition: Bullying behaviors happen more than once or have the potential to happen more than once.
>
> Bullying includes actions such as making threats, spreading rumors, attacking someone physically or verbally, and excluding someone from a group on purpose."

One University professor[1] suggests the following definition of bullying in general:

A desire to hurt **+ a hurtful action** **+ a power imbalance[2]** **+ repetition (typically)** **+ an unjust use of power** **+ evident enjoyment by the aggressor** **+ a sense of being oppressed on the part of the target**

Bullying can take place for our children anywhere and at any time.

It can take place before or during or after school. It can take place on a bus or carpool to and from school or while traveling to or from school activities. It can take place on the playground or at lunch. It can take place in the neighborhood, at parties, in shopping malls, or anywhere our children hang out.

As parents, we worry about how our children are treated each day and the "threats" and fears that they must face. As parents we should also be concerned that our kids are not just the victims of bullying but that our kids are not themselves bullies.

Bullies in ANY Form should not be tolerated by anyone

As will be seen, cyberbullying is just the natural modern-day extension of the pre-existing world of "ordinary" bullying.

---

[1] Ken Rigby, *Defining Bullying: A New Look at an Old Concept.* University of South Australia, Underdale Campus, July 2003.

[2] A **power imbalance** may be characterized by:
- Physical characteristics (age, size, strength)
- Popularity or association with popular peers
- Background/demographic characteristics (member of majority/minority group, socio-economic status
- Abilities and skills (academic, physical, artistic)
- Being outnumbered
- Presence of weapons

This book addresses and is designed make parents more aware that bullying in general has been expanded as to where and how it can take place, the extent of its reach and the severity of its impact.

For the most part, as reflected by the United States Department of Health and Human Services, ordinary bullying is found in three general categories:

"**Verbal bullying** is saying or writing mean things. Verbal bullying includes:

- Teasing
- Name-calling
- Inappropriate sexual comments
- Taunting
- Threatening to cause harm

Social bullying, sometimes referred to as relational bullying, involves hurting someone's reputation or relationships. Social bullying includes:

- Leaving someone out on purpose
- Telling other children not to be friends with someone
- Spreading rumors about someone
- Embarrassing someone in public

Physical bullying involves hurting a person's body or possessions. Physical bullying includes:

- Hitting/kicking/pinching
- Spitting
- Tripping/pushing
- Taking or breaking someone's things
- Making mean or rude hand gestures"

What Is Harassment?

Some believe that there is no or little difference between bullying and harassment, but in the eyes of the law, they are very different things.

So what is harassment? Each State has its own definition of the term, but a look at California definitions related to harassment are informative and typical:

> "'**Harassment**' is unlawful violence, a credible threat of violence, or a knowing and willful course of conduct directed at a specific person that seriously alarms, annoys, or harasses the person, and that serves no legitimate purpose. The course of conduct must be such as would cause a reasonable person to suffer substantial emotional distress, and must actually cause substantial emotional distress to the petitioner."[3]
>
> "'**Credible threat of violence**' is a knowing and willful statement or course of conduct that would place a reasonable person in fear for his or her safety, or the safety of his or her immediate family, and that serves no legitimate purpose."[4]
>
> "'**Course of conduct**' is a pattern of conduct composed of a series of acts over a period of time, however short, evidencing a continuity of purpose, including following or stalking an individual, making harassing telephone calls to an individual, or sending harassing correspondence to an individual by any means, including, but not limited to, the use of public or private mails, interoffice mail, facsimile, or computer email. Constitutionally protected activity is not included within the meaning of "course of conduct."[5]

For the most part, harassment involves forms of discrimination where bullying could but need not involve discrimination.

While there are similarities and overlap between the two concepts of abuse to our children, there may be a difference as to whether such conduct constitutes a violation of State and/or Federal law – and ultimately, what might be done about it.

---

[3] California Civil Code, Section 527.6(b)(3).

[4] California Civil Code, Section 527.6(b)(2).

[5] California Civil Code, Section 527.6(b)(1).

Quite simply, there are no current Federal laws against bullying but many States are starting to deal with this problem. In fact, the official government site for anti-bullying, stopbullying.gov[6], shows an interactive map of the United States, where you can find out about laws in your particular State against bullying.

The law is more clear about harassment when the harassment is based on a person's race, color, national origin, sex, disability, or religion – the violation now rises to a violation of Federal Civil Rights. Again, many States provide the same sorts of protections.

The bottom line, is that whether it is bullying or harassment that is at issue, it must not be allowed to exist.

Later in this book, we will deal with some of the laws related to harassment and bullying and some of things that might be done whenever there is any sort of bullying or harassment.

---

[6] Source, United States Department of Health & Human Services Stopbullying.gov website.

Chapter 3

OUR KIDS DON'T LIVE WITH US: THEY LIVE IN A CYBER WORLD

A Brief History Of Our Kids' Cyber World

In order to better appreciate and deal with cyberbullying, we must first understand the Cyber World of our kids. Our kids are intimately tied to social media – plugged in if you will. It is their lifeblood and it is their social world.

Social media is the online interaction among people in which they create, share or exchange information. Remarkably, social media is actually relatively new.

> Unlike us –
> our kids have never known
> a world without digital
> technology

One of the first social media web sites was Geocities which was created in 1994. It was a site that allowed its users to create their own web sites, characterized by one of six "cities" with different characteristics. The site was ultimately purchased by Yahoo! and shuttered in 2009. From Geocities, the world of social media took off.

- From 1997 through 2006 there were early social media sites such as SixDegrees and Blogger and Friendster

- Google was founded in September 1998

- In 2003 the corporate social media site LinkedIn opened, then MySpace that same year.

- On February 4, 2004 Facebook entered the scene

- Gmail was born on April 1, 2004

- YouTube opened shop one year later in February 2005 and was ultimately purchased by Google in November 2006

- Twitter started tweeting in March 2006

- Tumblr came on the scene in February 2007

- WhatsApp started in 2009

- Pinterest was first launched in March 2010 and Instagram that same year

Interestingly, Facebook initially was open only to Harvard students, then expanded to 800 colleges and by September 2006, Facebook was available to all users 13 and over.

> Our kids have unprecedented access to information
>
> And to other people

In April 2008, Facebook became more popular than MySpace and by December 2, 2009, Facebook membership hit 350 million. The climb in the popularity of Facebook continued and by July 2010 Facebook had over a half a billion users. Facebook became so popular that in March 2010, Facebook's weekly traffic surpassed that of Google.

In July 2011, LinkedIn became the #2 social media site in the United States with a total of 33.9 million monthly visitors. Twitter that same month celebrated its fifth year online by delivering over 350 million tweets per day.

Then in 2010, something happened that changed the course of the Cyber World and the belief that all was secure. On May 21, 2010 it was revealed that MySpace, Facebook and other social networks were sending user names and IDs to advertisers along with user URL data.

Currently, most people are aware of the security problems and invasions of privacy that are taking place daily in the country, and the need for action. And at very least, that action should be by parents for their children.

How Pervasive Is Social Media?

Internet usage and the use of social media in our country and around the world has become a normal and pervasive part of our daily life and the lives of our children.

How pervasive you may ask? You probably already think that your children are online all the time and possibly too much. By the fact that you are reading this book, you are probably already concerned that the amount of time spent online poses potential risks to your children. A better appreciation of the average online and social media usage in our country might help put in context the experience of you and your children.

Here are some interesting facts[7] that show us just how pervasive social networking and use of social media really is today. With regard to just the use of a social networking site, in 2015:

- 75% of all internet users use a social networking site

---

[7] Source: Pew Research Center report on *Social Media Usage: 2005-2015* and Pew Research Center report on *Teen, Social Media & Technology Overview 2015*.

- 65% of Adults use a social networking site (a nearly 10-fold jump in the past 10 years!)

- 90% of young adults (ages 18-29) use social media

- 94% of teens (ages 13-17) report going online daily. 24% of those teems say they are online "almost constantly"!

The sheer number of users on social networking is staggering. The following sampling of numbers provides a pretty clear indication of just how much social media permeates everyone's lives:

Facebook is by far the most popular social media site. There are about 1.6 billion monthly active users. The number of daily active users is over 1 billion![8]

To give this some perspective, consider that as of February 2016, the world population was estimated to be about 7.4 billion people. This means that in any given month, about 22% of the world's population uses Facebook!

In fact, the number of people who use Facebook every month, is more than the population of China.

The reach and impact of Facebook is so large, that it has over 3 million advertisers[9] who reach out to Facebook users.

In February 2016, the number of monthly Gmail users surpassed 1 billion.

In fact, other Google services have already reached the same mark of over 1 billion users per month. Those services include Search, Chrome, Android, Google Play, Maps and YouTube

Also in February 2016, WhatsApp users reached a new high of 1 billion people every month.

---

[8] Source, DMR, January 2016.

[9] Source, USA Today and Facebook, March, 2016.

The number of people who use Twitter is approximately 320 million. The number of active daily Twitter users is about 100 million.[10] There are approximately 340 million Tweets every day[11].

The number of people who use Instagram each month is approximately 400 million. More than 75 million use the service each day.[12]

Tinder users amount to about 50 million with about 10 million using the service daily.[13]

In terms of popularity, Psychology Today[14] reported in January 2016, that the top seven social networking sites used by teens, in order of popularity, are: Facebook, Instagram, Snapchat, Twitter, Google+, Vine and Tumblr.

As of the writing of this book, other social media sites that are on the rise include: Kik Messenger, ooVoo, YouNow, Burn Note, Whisper, Yik Yak, MeetMe, Omegle, Skout and Tinder[15].

One-in-three youth feel more accepted on social media than they do in real life!

McAfee for Business, 2014 Teens and the Screen study: Exploring Online Privacy, Social Networking and Cyberbullying

A new app to keep an eye on and be leery of is Peeple, an app allowing anyone to rate people, just like business are rated on Yelp.

---

[10] Source, DMR, October 2015.

[11] Source, Internet Live Stats, February 2016.

[12] Source, DMR, January 2016.

[13] Source DMR March, 2015.

[14] Source, Psychology Today, January 24, 2016 article by Raychelle Cassada Lohmann MS, LPC, entitled: *Top Five Social Networking Sites Used by Teens*. The article also referred to the Pew Research Center's report on *Teens, Social Media & Technology Overview 2015*.

[15] Source, Common Sense Media, March 4, 2015.

How Much Time is Spent On Social Media?

CNN reported[16] that teens spend a "mind boggling" 9 hours a day using media[17]! That's more time than the average teen sleeps!

The Pew Research Center's Internet Project[18] reported that: one-fifth of all Americans report going online "almost constantly"!

Our Kids are intimately tied into social media
– plugged in if you will –

It is their lifeblood and it is their social world

And let us not forget that our kids' smartphones are also a major gateway to social media.

It has been reported that Americans check their social media accounts 17 times a day and overall spend a staggering 4.7 hours a day on the phone[19].

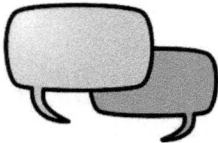

The statistics on text usage are almost unbelievable. 81% of cell phone owners send or receive text messages[20]. 91% of teens use text messaging.[21]

The average teen sends and receives 30 texts per day. That amounts to 10,950 texts per year! Teen boys send an average of 20 texts per day, while teen girls send an average of 40 texts per day.

---

[16] CNN November 3, 2015.

[17] "Media" includes non-internet media such as TV and radio.

[18] Pew Research Internet Project Fact Sheet,

[19] Source, Informate Mobile Intelligence.

[20] Source: Pew Research Center report on *Social Media Usage: 2005-2015* and Pew Research Center report on *Teen, Social Media & Technology Overview 2015*.

[21] Source: Pew Research Center report on *Social Media Usage: 2005-2015* and Pew Research Center report on *Teen, Social Media & Technology Overview 2015*.

Older teen girls (ages 15-17) send an average of 50 texts per day or 18,250 texts per year! [22]

Getting back to how much time is spent on just a couple of social media sites, Businessweek and Bloomberg Business on July 23, 2014 reported that:

- Facebook says the average American spends 40 minutes a day checking a Facebook feed.

So how does that compare to other time spent by the average person? It's actually greater than most activities![23]

- Average time spent taking care of pets: 39 minutes

- Average time spent buying consumer goods: 39 minutes

- Average time spent traveling to work: 35 minutes

- Average time doing housework: 34 minutes

- Average time spent on household and personal e-mail: 33 minutes

- Average time spent on household and personal snail-mail: 17 minutes

- Average time spent participating in organizational, civic, or religious activities: 14 minutes

- Caring for and helping household children: 11 minutes

- Average time spent participating in sports, exercise and recreation: 9 minutes

---

[22] Source: Pew Research Center report on *Social Media Usage: 2005-2015* and Pew Research Center report on *Teen, Social Media & Technology Overview 2015*.

[23] Source, United States Bureau of Labor Statistics, Economic News Release.

eMarketer reported the following average daily time spent on select social medial sites for youth between the ages of 18-29[24]:

- 51 minutes for Facebook
- 29.9 minutes for Instagram
- 23.5 minutes for Twitter
- 19.8 minutes for Snapchat

REMEMBER:

Unlike us, our kids' social world IS the internet and social media!

When one looks at just the relatively few statistics provided in this chapter, is there any wonder that the social world of our kids is dominated by the Cyber World and social media?

Is there any wonder that parents need to be concerned about and know the Cyber World that their children live in?

---

[24] Source, eMarketer, November 18, 2014.

Chapter 4

WHAT IS CYBERBULLYING?

We now need to turn to the inevitable intersection of the Cyber World of social media with "ordinary" bullying and harassment: cyberbullying.

What Is Cyberbullying?

The United States Department of Health & Human Services defines cyberbullying as:

> "Cyberbullying is bullying that takes place using electronic technology. Electronic technology includes devices and equipment such as cell phones, computers, and tablets as well as communication tools including social media sites, text messages, chat, and websites.
>
> "Examples of cyberbullying include mean text messages or emails, rumors sent by email or posted on social networking sites, and embarrassing pictures, videos, websites, or fake profiles"[25]

Cyberbullying is usually defined in legal glossaries as:

- Actions that use information and communication technologies to support deliberate, repeated, and hostile behavior by an individual or group, that is intended to harm another or others
- Use of communication technologies for the intention of harming another person
- Use of internet service and mobile technologies such as web pages and discussion groups as well as instant messaging or SMS text messaging with the intention of harming another person

---

[25] Source, United States Department of Health & Human Services Stopbullying.gov website.

Our kids need to be aware of and sensitive to the fact
that what they may believe is just harmless fun or
teasing, may very well result in or be viewed as
harassment to the victim

What Makes Cyberbullying Different Than "Regular" Bullying And Harassment?

The United States Department of Health & Human Services makes it clear why cyberbullying is different:

"Kids who are being cyberbullied are often bullied in person as well. Additionally, kids who are cyberbullied have a harder time getting away from the behavior."

• Cyberbullying can happen 24 hours a day, 7 days a week, and reach a kid even when he or she is alone. It can happen any time of the day or night.

• Cyberbullying messages and images can be posted anonymously and distributed quickly to a very wide audience. It can be difficult and sometimes impossible to trace the source.

• Deleting inappropriate or harassing messages, texts, and pictures is extremely difficult after they have been posted or sent." [26]

In essence, cyberbullying is ordinary bullying and harassment magnified. The reason is that the Cyber World and most social media are widespread and accessible to all, immediately accessible and public to a massive audience of users, permanent (once something is on the internet and in social media, it seems to never go away) and anonymous.

---

[26] Source, United States Department of Health & Human Services Stopbullying.gov website.

Anonymity is a shield for a bully that does not exist in the world outside of the Cyber World. Anonymity allows a bully to be free from ordinary social restraint.

How Is Cyberbullying Done?

Cyberbullying can take place in various forms over the various types of Social Media. But in general, it takes place in these categories:

- **Direct Attacks**

  - Are hurtful messages sent from the cyber bully directly to the target through email, social networking sites, instant messaging, or other forums

  - Might be anonymous or sent through fake accounts, often targeting the victim relentlessly

- **Indirect Attacks Or Campaigns**

  - Are widespread messages that hurt the victim's reputation

  - May involve cyber bullies starting a website or a page on a social networking site dedicated to spreading hateful messages about the victim

- **Invasions of Privacy**

  - Involve the cyber bully going through the victim's computer or cell phone in order to find private emails, text messages, or photos and then sharing those personal details or pictures with others

  - Include secretly leaving a webcam running and recording the target's actions without their knowledge

o   May also entail installing spyware on the target's computer.

How Prevalent Is Cyberbullying?

There has always been bullying. And parents have always been concerned that their child was either the victim of bullying or participated in bullying. And given the sheer numbers of social interactions available to our children through the internet and social media, whether voluntary or otherwise, is there any wonder that the bully would take advantage of the ease and anonymity offered?

> Cyberbullying is really just the modern day equivalent of bullying and harassment
>
> On steroids!

But could any of us have predicted just how prevalent cyberbullying would become?

Fortunately, there is a plethora of statistics involving bullying and cyberbullying – but most of the statistics aren't always clear on the distinction between the two. So the reader is asked to be understanding of the fact that the author is not making too much of a distinction between the types of bullying our youth experience, and is merely trying to present some of the available studies and statistics to give the reader an idea of the extent of the problem.

However, no matter the type of bullying– it is all still bullying that is extensive and pervasive and in need of being stopped.

A study was conducted by McAfee in 2014[27] which reported that 87% of youth have witnessed cyberbullying.

---

[27] McAfee for Business "Cyberbullying Triples" article June 3, 2014.

The United States Department of Education has reported that at least 22% of students aged 12-18 were bullied in the 2012-2013 school year.[28] Nearly 1 out of every 4 kids has been a victim!

The United States Centers for Disease Control, reports that in the 2013 school year, about 20% of students experienced cyberbullying[29].

52% of lesbian, gay, bisexual and transgender youth report experiencing bullying.[30]

Of victims who reported they were cyberbullied, 72% reported that it was due to appearance, while 26% noted it was due to race or religion, and 22% indicated that their sexuality was the driving factor.[31]

Nearly 1 out of 4 kids have been the victim of bullying

And

Nearly 1 out of 5 kids have been the victim of cyberbullying

Spreading rumors online or through text messages seems to be the most common type of cyberbullying. The next most common form of cyberbullying includes posting mean or hurtful comments or pictures, followed by actual threats to hurt someone. Following right behind these types of cyberbullying is pretending to be someone else online and being mean and hurtful to others. Approximately 5.5% of the kids surveyed admitted to doing one or

[28] Source, United States Department of Education, report from the 2013 School Crime Supplement (SCS) of the National Crime Victimization Survey (NCVS).

[29] Source, Centers for Disease Control, *Morbidity and Mortality Weekly Report, June 13, 2014, on Youth Risk Behavior Surveillance – United States, 2013*.

[30] Kosciw, J. G., Greytak, E. A., Bartkiewicz, M. J., Boesen, M. J., & Palmer, N. A. (2012). *The 2011 National School Climate Survey: The experiences of lesbian, gay, bisexual and transgender youth in our nation's schools.* New York: GLSEN.

[31] McAfee for Business, *2014 Teens and the Screen study: Exploring Online Privacy, Social Networking and Cyberbullying.*

more of these forms of cyberbullying two or more times during the course of the 30 days prior to the survey.[32]

According to one large study, the following percentages of middle school students had experienced various types of bullying: name calling (44.2 %), teasing (43.3 %), spreading rumors or lies (36.3%), pushing or shoving (32.4%), hitting, slapping, or kicking (29.2%), being left out (28.5%), threatening (27.4%), stealing belongings (27.3%), sexual comments or gestures (23.7%), e-mail or blogging (9.9%)[33].

Maybe of more concern, is that approximately 30% of young people admit in surveys to bullying others[34].

Most bullying seems to occur in middle school with the most common types being verbal and social bullying[35].

Approximately 30% of young people admit to bullying others!

In a Department of Education study, it appeared that only 39% of the students ever reported being bullied at school to an adult[36].

Another study earlier than that of the Department of Education, found that only about 20-30% of students who are bullied ever notify adults about the bullying[37].

---

[32] Source, Cyberbullying Research Center, February 2015 Cyberbullying by Gender.

[33] Bradshaw, C.P., Sawyer, A.L., & O'Brennan, L.M. (2007). Bullying and peer victimization at school: Perceptual differences between students and school staff. *School Psychology Review, 36*(3), 361-382

[34] Bradshaw, C.P., Sawyer, A.L., & O'Brennan, L.M. (2007). Bullying and peer victimization at school: Perceptual differences between students and school staff. *School Psychology Review, 36*(3), 361-382. As reported by stopbullying.gov.

[35] Source, United States Department of Health & Human Services Stopbullying.gov website.

[36] Source, United States Department of Education, report from the 2013 School Crime Supplement (SCS) of the National Crime Victimization Survey (NCVS).

[37] Ttofi, M.M., Farrington, D.P. (2011). Effectiveness of school-based programs to reduce bullying: a systematic and meta-analytic review. *Journal of Experimental Criminology,7*(1), 27-56.

It has been reported that every 7 minutes, a child is bullied and that 85% of the time there is no intervention by adults or peers in the bullying[38].

It is also estimated that about 160,000 children miss school every day due to fear of attack or intimidation by other students[39].

Somewhere between 61% to 70% of students don't even report the bullying to an adult

Who Is At Risk Of Being Cyberbullied?

It seems that there is no single factor that puts a particular child at risk of bullying or cyberbullying.

Bullying can and does happen everywhere and potentially to anyone.

We do know that adolescent girls have been found to be more likely to experience cyberbullying in their lifetimes than are boys. In fact, the difference in the percentages of girls experiencing cyberbullying over their lifetimes than boys is pronounced: 40.6% to 28.2%.[40].

Psychology Today[41] listed a number of factors associated with being the target of bullies. They include being "different" in some way, being competent and threatening to the bully, being nice and the type of person who won't fight back, and being socially isolated

---

[38] Source, National Voices for Equality Education and Enlightenment, Bullying Statistics.

[39] Source, National Education Association.

[40] Source, Cyberbullying Research Center, February 2015 Cyberbullying by Gender.

[41] Source, Psychology Today, January 3, 2013 article entitled: Are You an Easy Target for Bullies?

The United States Department of Health & Human Services has stated a few factors that appear to put a child at risk of being bullied:

> "Generally, children who are bullied have one or more of the following risk factors:
>
> - Are perceived as different from their peers, such as being overweight or underweight, wearing glasses or different clothing, being new to a school, or being unable to afford what kids consider "cool"
>
> - Are perceived as weak or unable to defend themselves
>
> - Are depressed, anxious, or have low self esteem
>
> - Are less popular than others and have few friends
>
> - Do not get along well with others, seen as annoying or provoking, or antagonize others for attention
>
> However, even if a child has these risk factors, it doesn't mean that they will be bullied."[42]

Children with disabilities are also at an increased risk of being bullied, and as previously mentioned, when the cyberbullying involves lesbian, gay, bisexual and transgender youth, the frequency of experiencing bullying has been reported to be as high as 52%[43].

Who Is More Likely To Bully Others?

First off we should be clear that male and female kids cyberbully about the same. A recent study reported that 15.5% of male school children surveyed said that they had cyberbullied others in their

---

[42] Source, United States Department of Health & Human Services Stopbullying.gov website.

[43] Kosciw, J. G., Greytak, E. A., Bartkiewicz, M. J., Boesen, M. J., & Palmer, N. A. (2012). *The 2011 National School Climate Survey: The experiences of lesbian, gay, bisexual and transgender youth in our nation's schools*. New York: GLSEN.

lifetimes[44]. In the same study it was found that 14% of female students surveyed said that they had cyberbullied others in their lifetimes.

The United States Department of Health & Human Services has reported a few factors that indicate the types of children who are more likely to bully others:

"There are two types of kids who are more likely to bully others:

- Some are well-connected to their peers, have social power, are overly concerned about their popularity, and like to dominate or be in charge of others

- Others are more isolated from their peers and may be depressed or anxious, have low self-esteem, be less involved in school, be easily pressured by peers, or not identify with the emotions or feelings of others

Children who have these factors are also more likely to bully others;

- Are aggressive or easily frustrated

- Have less parental involvement or having issues at home

- Think badly of others

- Have difficulty following rules

- View violence in a positive way

- Have friends who bully others

Remember, those who bully others do not need to be stronger or bigger than those they bully. The power imbalance can come from a number of sources—popularity, strength, cognitive ability—and children who bully may have more than one of these characteristics." [45]

[44] Source, Cyberbullying Research Center, February 2015 Cyberbullying by Gender.

[45] Source, United States Department of Health & Human Services Stopbullying.gov website.

Chapter 5

THE RAMIFICATIONS OF CYBERBULLYING
Understand the Problem

There is no question that cyberbullying is pervasive. Our instinct and experience with our own children tells us that the effect of cyberbullying or harassment (or any sort of bullying) is horrible and needs to be stopped.

But are you really aware of just how bad the ramifications of cyberbullying and bullying in general can be on our youth?

The Effects Of Cyberbullying On The Victim

Kids who are bullied have a greater chance of experiencing depression and anxiety for sure. The Centers for Disease Control also informs us that:

> "Bullying can result in physical injury, social and emotional distress, and even death. Victimized youth are at increased risk for depression, anxiety, sleep difficulties, and poor school adjustment. Youth who bully others are at increased risk for substance use, academic problems, and violence later in adolescence and adulthood. Compared to youth who only bully, or who are only victims, bully-victims suffer the most serious consequences and are at greater risk for both mental health and behavior problems." [46]

---

[46] Source, Centers for Disease Control, *Understanding Bullying, Fact Sheet 2015.*

A Yale University School of Medicine study in 2008 reportedly found that bullied victims are 7-9% more likely to consider suicide[47].

These sorts of statistics as well as some horrible stories in the news and anecdotal reports, have seemingly created in parents a profound concern that there is a real relationship between cyberbullying (or bullying in general) and suicide.

So is there a connection between cyberbullying and suicide? The short answer is that there probably is some sort of connection – but the nature and extent of that connection probably cannot be known other than that cyberbullying is an unquantifiable factor.

Suggestions that bullying is or could be a single, direct cause of suicide, is believed by the Centers for Disease Control as "not helpful and is potentially harmful because it could" (1) "perpetuate the false notion that suicide is a natural response to being bullied"; (2) "encourage sensationalized reporting"; (3) "focus the response on blame and punishment which misdirects the attention from getting the needed support and treatment" to victims and bullies; and (4) "take attention away from other important risk factors for suicidal behavior"

Source, Centers for Disease Control, National Center for Injury Prevention and Control Division of Violence Prevention, *The Relationship Between Bullying and Suicide: What we Know and What it Means for Schools*

---

[47] Source, Yale News July 16, 2008, *Bullying-Suicide Link Explored in New Study by Researchers at Yale.*

Let's briefly explore some of what is known and not known about whether there is a connection between cyberbullying and suicide – hopefully to assuage some of the fears of parents – but also to remind parents that they still need to be quite alert to what could be a bigger problem than we truly know or can prove at this time.

To start to understand the nature and extent of any connection between cyberbullying and suicide, we first turn to the Centers for Disease Control report on solely what is known about suicide (without considering bullying).

There we find that[48]:

> - "Suicide-related behavior is complicated and rarely the result of a single source of trauma or stress
>
> - People who engage in suicide-related behavior often experience overwhelming feelings of helplessness and hopelessness
>
> - ANY involvement with bullying behavior is one stressor which may significantly contribute to feelings of helplessness and hopelessness that raise the risk of suicide
>
> - Youth who are at increased risk for suicide-related behavior are dealing with a complex interaction of multiple relationship (peer, family, or romantic) mental health, and school stressors"[49]

Now as for "connecting" bullying and suicide, we need to understand what we do know about bullying and suicide together. And here again, we turn to what appears to be one of the more reliable sources of information - the studies conducted by the Centers for Disease Control.

---

[48] Source, Centers for Disease Control, National Center for Injury Prevention and Control Division of Violence Prevention, *The Relationship Between Bullying and Suicide: What we Know and What it Means for Schools.*

[49] Source, Centers for Disease Control, National Center for Injury Prevention and Control Division of Violence Prevention, *The Relationship Between Bullying and Suicide: What we Know and What it Means for Schools.*

> "We know that bullying behavior and suicide-related behavior are closely related. This means youth who report any involvement with bullying behavior are more likely to report high levels of suicide-related behavior than youth who do not report any involvement with bullying behavior.
>
> We know enough about the relationship between bullying and suicide-related behavior to make evidence-based recommendations to improve prevention efforts." [50]

And finally, as to what we do not know about the connection between bullying and suicide:

> "We don't know if bullying directly causes suicide-related behavior. We know that most youth who are involved in bullying do NOT engage in suicide-related behavior. It is correct to say that involvement in bullying, along with other risk factors, increases the chance that a young person will engage in suicide-related behaviors." [51]

Again, the most that we will likely be able to know is that there probably is some sort of connection, but the nature and extent of that connection is not currently understood. Cyberbullying is an unquantifiable factor.

Other circumstances that can affect a person's vulnerability to either cyberbullying or suicide are family, community and society. These factors can include: "emotional distress; exposure to violence; family conflict; relationship problems; lack of connectedness to school/sense of supportive school environment; alcohol and drug use; physical disabilities/learning differences; lack of access to resources/support." [52]

---

[50] Source, Centers for Disease Control, National Center for Injury Prevention and Control Division of Violence Prevention, *The Relationship Between Bullying and Suicide: What we Know and What it Means for Schools.*

[51] Source, Centers for Disease Control, National Center for Injury Prevention and Control Division of Violence Prevention, *The Relationship Between Bullying and Suicide: What we Know and What it Means for Schools.*

[52] Source, Centers for Disease Control, National Center for Injury Prevention and Control Division of Violence Prevention, *The Relationship Between Bullying and Suicide: What we Know and What it Means for Schools.*

So if cyberbullying can be and probably is some sort of a factor in the risk of suicide, we should have an appreciation of the extent of the suicide problem for our youth. According to the American Academy of Child and Adolescent Psychiatry and the Centers for Disease Control, suicide is the third leading cause of death for youth aged 15-24.

The United States Department of Health & Human Services has reported a few results of bullying on the victim:

> "Kids who are bullied can experience negative physical, school, and mental health issues. Kids who are bullied are more likely to experience:
>
> - Depression and anxiety, increased feelings of sadness and loneliness, changes in sleep and eating patterns, and loss of interest in activities they used to enjoy. These issues may persist into adulthood.
>
> - Health complaints
>
> - Decreased academic achievement – GPA and standardized test scores – and school participation. They are more likely to miss, skip, or drop out of school.
>
> A very small number of bullied children might retaliate through extremely violent measures. In 12 of 15 school shooting cases in the 1990s, the shooters had a history of being bullied. [53]

The California Department of Education has stated that

> "Students who are the target of a bully experience negative emotions. Feelings of persecution prevail over feelings of safety and confidence. Fear, anger, frustration, and anxiety may lead to ongoing illness, mood swings, withdrawal from friends and family, an inability to concentrate, and loss of interest in school. If left unattended, the targeted student may develop attendance and/or discipline problems, fail at school altogether or, in the worst cases, they are suicidal or retaliatory and violent. [54]

---

[53] Source, United States Department of Health & Human Services Stopbullying.gov website.

[54] Source, California Department of education, *Bullying at School.*

The former chancellor of Washington D.C.'s public school system estimated that more than 160,000 students are absent from school each day because they are afraid of bullying in general.[55]. This amounts to nearly 3.5 million kids per month!

The Diagnostic and Statistic Manual (DSM) which all doctors use to diagnose mental illness, recognizes that in the case of trauma such as bullying, the result can be Post Traumatic Stress Disorder (PTSD). The DSM recognizes that PTSD can be caused ty an "accumulation of many small, individually non-life-threatening incidents". A study by Hasbro Children's Hospital in Rhode Island found widespread cyberbullying and signs of PTSD among teens.

There is no question that cyberbullying has and can have profound negative effects on the victim.

There is no question that cyberbullying must be considered a very serious problem that parents should not take lightly.

The Effects Of Cyberbullying On The Bully

Lest one forget, there are also ramifications of bullying on the bully.

The California Department of Education has stated that

> "Without support or intervention, students who bully will continue to bully and may engage in other types of antisocial behavior and crime. Although some students who bully are less likely to be trusted and may be seen as mean and manipulative, a bully who learns aggression toward others garners power and may find the behavior a difficult habit to break. Some acts of bullying result in suspension or expulsion of students and translate into child abuse and domestic violence in adulthood. Research shows that 60 percent of males who bully in grades six through nine are convicted of at least one crime as adults, compared with 23 percent of males who did not bully." [56]

[55] Source, The Atlantic, October 3, 2013 article: *160,000 Kids Stay Home From School Each Day To Avoid Being Bullied.*

[56] Source, California Department of education, *Bullying at School.*

The Attorney General of California in 2011[57] reported that:

- Bullying is linked to delinquency

- Bullies are more likely to get into fights

- Bullies are more likely to carry weapons

- Bullies are more likely to be convicted of a crime by the age of 24

The United States Department of Health & Human Services has reported a few results of bullying on the bully:

> "Kids who bully others can also engage in violent and other risky behaviors into adulthood. Kids who bully are more likely to:
>
> - Abuse alcohol and other drugs in adolescence and as adults
>
> - Get into fights, vandalize property, and drop out of school
>
> - Engage in early sexual activity
>
> - Have criminal convictions and traffic citations as adults
>
> - Be abusive toward their romantic partners, spouses, or children as adults"[58]

The Effects Of Cyberbullying On The Bystander

Even those who passively witness cyberbullying can be impacted.

The California Department of Education has addressed this often-times ignored issue when it stated:

---

[57] Source, Mercury News, November 15, 2011.

[58] Source, United States Department of Health & Human Services Stopbullying.gov website.

"Students who passively participate in bullying by watching may come to believe that the behavior is acceptable and that the adults at school either do not care enough or are powerless to stop it. Some students may join in with the bully; others who share common traits with the target may fear they will become the next target. Research indicates that witnesses to bullying develop a loss of their sense of security which can reduce learning." [59]

---

[59] Source, California Department of education, *Bullying at School*.

Chapter 6

THERE'S NO PRIVACY IN THE CYBER WORLD

How Private Is The Cyber World?

Don't forget that our "smart" cell phones are also part of the Cyber World, and they are constantly delivering data on each of us to third parties.

The Wall Street Journal reported in March 2015 about a Carnegie Mellon University study that found "a dozen or so popular Android apps collected device location – GPS coordinates accurate to within 50 meters – an average 6,200 times, or roughly every three minutes per participant over a two-week period."

> Any belief that there is any privacy in the Cyber World
>
> IS ABSOLUTELY WRONG!

The same study found that the Weather Channel for example, requested location information an average 2,000 times, or every 10 minutes during the study. Even Groupon requested one participant's coordinates 1,062 times in the same two weeks.

If you actually examine the permissions you grant the apps on your smart phone, you would probably be quite shocked to know that you have agreed to allow all sorts of apps permissions to look at and use virtually all of the private information on your smartphone!

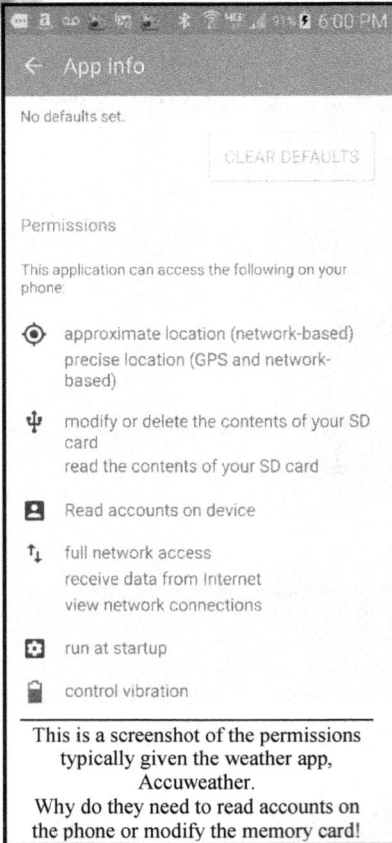

This is a screenshot of the permissions typically given the weather app, Accuweather.
Why do they need to read accounts on the phone or modify the memory card!

The permissions generally given to apps include the right to read contacts as well as sensitive log information! Some apps can send SMS messages or read social media streams. In fact, the permissions granted to some apps have gone so far as to allow them to wipe out data on your smartphone!

Too often, when an app is added to our smart phone, we install them without any thought as to privacy.

It seems that most people when installing apps don't read the permission requests during the installation process. They just click on anything that says "yes" or "I agree", mindless of the privacy they have given away and lost.

Oftentimes, the only way to install a desired app, is to agree to anything that is required for the installation, and most of us will agree.

While Google has recently updated its Android operating system to "Marshmallow" which now allows the user to limit or modify permissions[60], still most users don't take advantage of the opportunity to limit the use of their data.

It is shocking just how much data is collected on us all while using the internet.

---

[60] We will take a look at this new Android function later in the book.

Each time we are on the internet, we are unwittingly sharing important information about ourselves with others.

But the lack of privacy extends even further.

Our kids are unwittingly sharing information when they use the internet and are on social media sites. Worse still as we will see a little later, our kids are also voluntarily and mindlessly handing over their personal information online without regard to the ramifications of doing so.

Just take a look at these screen shots from Google, setting forth the main types of information and data Google collects when we use any of its services[61]:

As you can see, just using Google devices means you are sharing much of your personal information whether you really want to or not.

What data does Google collect?

Here are the main types of information we collect.

Things you do

When you use our services — for example, do a search on Google, get directions on Google Maps, or watch a video on YouTube — we collect basic information to make these services work. This can include:

- Things you search for
- Websites you visit
- Videos you watch
- Ads you click on or tap
- Your location
- Device information
- IP address and cookie data

---

[61] Source: Google Website screen capture on January 27, 2016.

And if that weren't enough, here is still more that you share with Google!

Knowing that every online search and website visited can be shared with others without you being aware it is happening and without your agreement each time it takes place – is frightening for most

Things that make you "you"

When you sign up for a Google Account, we keep the basic information you give us. This can include your:

- Name
- Email address and password
- Birthday
- Gender
- Phone number
- Country

If you have given us your billing information in order to make a purchase, we securely store it on our servers, just like we do with your basic information.

Things you create

If you are signed in with your Google Account, we store and protect what you create using our services, so you will always have your information when you need it. This can include:

- Emails you send and receive on Gmail
- Contacts you add
- Calendar events
- Photos and videos you upload
- Docs, Sheets, and Slides on Drive

Just imagine where else and how much your personal data and interests and even your location are being shared with others.

Actually, don't imagine – know that YOUR DATA IS BEING SHARED!

How Private Are Your Kids?
What Do They Share With Others?

Teens are sharing more information about themselves on social media sites than they have in the past[62].

- 92% post their real name

- 91% post a photo of themselves. Older teens post their photo 94% of the time

- 84% post their interests

- 82% post their birth date.

- 71% post their school name. Older teens post this information 76% of the time

- 71% post the city or town

- 62% post their relationship status. Older teens post their status 66% of the time.

- 53% post their email address

- 24% post videos of themselves.

- 20% post their cell phone number. Older teens post their number 23% of the time.

- 64% of teens with Twitter accounts make their tweets public

[62] Source, Pew Research Center, *Teens, Social Media, and Privacy*, May 21, 2013.

- 12% of teens with Twitter accounts don't even know if their tweets are public

- 40% of teens with Facebook accounts keep their profiles public

- 33% of Facebook friends for teens are people they have not met in person

Our kids are not just involuntarily sharing personal information

They are actually choosing to share personal and confidential information

Chapter 7

WARNING SIGNS OF CYBERBULLYING

Don't forget that most kids don't even report that they are the victims of or have experienced bullying to an adult.

As a result, we adults need to actively look for signs of cyberbullying to be as sure as we can to pick up the need for stopping and/or remedying cyberbullying.

At least 61% to 70% of students don't even report bullying to an adult

<u>Warning Signs That A Child Is A Victim Of Cyberbullying</u>

Here are some generally recognized signs that may point to the existence of a bullying problem:[63]

- Unexplainable injuries

- Lost or destroyed clothing, books, electronics, or other personal items

- Frequent headaches or stomachaches, feeling sick or faking illness

---

[63] Source: The National Center on Safe Supportive Learning Environments (NCSSLE) is funded by the U.S. Department of Education's Office of Safe and Healthy Students.

- Changes in eating habits, like suddenly skipping meals or binge eating; alternatively, children may come home from school hungry because they did not eat lunch

- Difficulty sleeping or frequent nightmares

- Declining grades, loss of interest in schoolwork, or not wanting to go to school

- Sudden loss of friends or avoidance of social situations

- Feeling of helplessness or decreased self-esteem

- Self-destructive behaviors such as running away from home, harming themselves, or talking about suicide

Some of the generally accepted suicide warning signs can also be signs of bullying and cyberbullying[64]:

- Talking about wanting to die or to kill oneself

- Looking for a way to kill oneself, such as search online or buying a gun

- Talking about feeling hopeless or having no reason to live

- Talking about feeling trapped or in unbearable pain

- Talking about being a burden to others

- Increasing the use of alcohol or drugs

- Acting anxious or agitated, behaving recklessly

---

[64] From the State of California Department of Justice Office of the Attorney General.

- Sleeping too little or too much

- Withdrawing or feeling isolated

- Showing rage or talking about seeking revenge

- Displaying extreme mood swings

Needless to say, any of these signs of bullying or its psychological impact should alert parents to further explore whether there is a problem and whether a child needs assistance. Signs of a problem may not mean there is a problem, but ignoring these signs could be a tragic mistake.

Warning Signs That A Child Is Bullying Others

Here are some generally recognized signs that may point to the existence of a bullying problem[65]:

- Getting into physical or verbal fights

- Having friends who bully others

- Becoming increasingly aggressive

- Getting sent to the principal's office or to detention frequently

- Having unexplained extra money or new belongings

- Blaming others for their problems

- Not accepting responsibility for their actions

[65] From: The National Center on Safe Supportive Learning Environments (NCSSLE) is funded by the U.S. Department of Education's Office of Safe and Healthy Students.

- Being competitive and worrying about their reputation or popularity

Chapter 8

THERE ARE FEDERAL AND STATE PROTECTIONS AGAINST CYBERBULLYING

Federal Laws

Unfortunately, as of the writing of this book, there are no Federal laws that specifically address cyberbullying. While legislation has been proposed in the House of Representatives[66], it has not yet passed.

There are both Federal and State laws that can help you protect your child

Look into them when needed

However, if the bullying is based on race, national origin, color, sex, age, disability or religion – then what we are talking about are Civil Rights violation for which a number of laws are in place.

Some of the applicable laws in place for civil rights violations include:

- Title IV and Title VI of the Civil Rights Act of 1964

    o Bar discrimination based on race, color or national origin in any program or activity that receives federal financial assistance. They also prohibit discrimination in public schools based upon a student's religious beliefs

---

[66] The Megan Meier Cyberbullying Prevention Act was introduced in the House of Representatives in 2009.

- Title IX of the Education Amendments of 1972

  - Bans discrimination on the basis of sex or gender in educational programs and activities receiving federal funding. Unless it's an all-boys or all-girls school, it can't deny admission to a student simply because he's of the opposite sex. It also covers sexual harassment by staff and other students. There's some debate, however, about if and when Title IX applies to discrimination based on sexual orientation, such as when a gay or lesbian student is the victim of discrimination

- Section 504 of the Rehabilitation Act of 1973

  - Makes it illegal for any program and activity that gets federal money to discriminate against somebody based upon a disability. "Disability" includes many physical and mental or psychological disabilities

- Titles II and III of the Americans with Disabilities Act

  - Ban discrimination based on disabilities. Disabilities include both mental and physical medical conditions. A condition does not need to be severe or permanent to be a disability

- Individuals with Disabilities Education Act

  - Makes sure that children with disabilities have the opportunity to receive a free, appropriate public education, just like other children. The Act requires that special education and related services be made available to every eligible child with a disability

A federally funded school (including primary and secondary schools as well as colleges and universities) has an obligation to resolve harassment problems.

What are those schools' obligations for harassment involving protected classes? Those obligations are listed in Chapter 11 relating to the obligations of schools.

Suffice it to say for now, that in the event that a school does not resolve the problem, recourse could be had through the U.S. Department of Education's Office for Civil Rights and the U.S. Department of Justice's Civil Rights Division.

Please understand that this book is not attempting to provide legal advice to you or to be exhaustive in what laws might apply to your particular situation. All that is attempted here, is to give you some sense that laws do exist to provide additional protections to you and your children when needed. In all cases, you need to consult with appropriate counsel and/or your own attorney for proper legal advice.

State Laws

As of the writing of this book, every State has laws related to ordinary bullying. And with the exception of Alaska and Wisconsin, the other 48 states also protect against electronic forms of harassment.

For the most part, again depending on State, all of the State laws that relate to only ordinary bullying/harassment can usually be extended to cover, in some form or the other, cyberbullying.

There are 24 States that have specific laws regarding cyberbullying.

Every State with the exception of Montana, requires school policies dealing with bullying. Interestingly, 13 of those States include in their school policies not only on-campus behaviours, but also off-campus behaviors. In other words, a school might be empowered or even mandated, to expel a student for off-campus cyberbullying.

In addition to the civil laws related to bullying and cyberbullying in all of the States, 18 of those States also provide for criminal sanctions for bullying.

While the laws of each State are different, a quick look at the criminal laws in California is illustrative of the types of prohibitions and punishment that exist for cyberbullying and bullying in general:

Two types of online or electronic conduct can be found to be crimes in California:

1.   Electronically posting personal identifying date of another person or a harassing message about another person, with the intent to cause the other person to reasonably fear for his or her safety or the safety of family members commits a misdemeanor crime[67].

2.   Any person who uses a telephone or any electronic means of communication to contact another person and uses obscene language or makes a threat to injure the person or property of the other person or a family member with the intent to annoy the other person commits a misdemeanor crime[68].

Punishment for these misdemeanors if convicted, can include a jail sentence of not more than one year in jail, a fine of not more than $1,000, or both[69].

California also makes hate motivated conduct a crime that can be punished by a jail sentence of not more than one year in jail, a fine of not more than $5,000, or both[70].

As you can see, cyberbullying can result in criminal penalties as well as civil liability to the victim in a civil lawsuit.

Your State probably has in place laws that can provide significant protections against and penalties applicable to cyberbullying.

---

[67] California Penal Code § 653.2.

[68] California Penal Code § 653m.

[69] California Penal Code § 653.2.

[70] California Penal Code § 422.6.

You should do a little research to see what your State offers you by way of protection.

As usual, please understand that this book is not attempting to provide legal advice to you or to be exhaustive in what laws might apply to your particular situation. All that is attempted here, is to give you some sense that laws do exist to provide additional protection to you and your children when needed. In all cases, you need to consult with appropriate counsel and/or your own attorney for proper legal advice.

Chapter 9

LIABILITY OF A BULLY:
It Doesn't Matter If He Or She Is A Minor!

Contrary to popular (or is that hopeful) belief, your minor child can be sued for his or her actions as a cyberbully.

Only very young children (usually those under 4 years of age) will generally not be found liable for their conduct. For the most part, they are not considered to have the mental capacity or understanding to be held responsible for the actions.

For the most part, children older than 4 can be held legally liable for their conduct. Usually, that child would have to be found to be old enough to form an intent to commit the harm. From 4 – 14 years of age there is generally a presumption that the child can not form the requisite intent – but the presumption is

> For the most part, a minor is NOT immune from liability and may be sued

rebuttable and a child could be found capable of being held legally responsible. Older than 14 years old, a child is generally presumed to be able to form the intent to be held liable.

Under the Federal Rules of Civil Procedure, all that is necessary to sue a minor, is to do so through a legal representative for that minor. The courts are concerned that the interests of a minor being sued are protected by an adult, thus the requirement of a legal representative during the litigation. Generally the adult involved on behalf of the minor is a parent or a conservator or a representative appointed by the court..[71]

---

[71] See Federal Rules of Civil Procedure, Section 17.

Likewise, most States have laws in place that allow a minor to be sued for conduct that is legally improper.

In addition to being subject to the Federal and State laws related to bullying and cyberbullying, there are also non-statutory common law legal harms that a minor could be found liable for.

A minor could be sued by the victim and potentially be found liable for a variety of causes of action including, but not limited to:

- Assault

- Defamation

- Harassment

- Hate crimes

- Injunctions

- Invasion of privacy

- Intentional Infliction of Emotional Distress

- Negligent Infliction of Emotional Distress

- Negligence and Breach of the Duty of Due Care

- Violations of Civil Rights

Liability for these civil wrongs could result in money damages assessed against the child for any and all monetary damages suffered by the victim.

Again, please understand that this book is not attempting to provide legal advice to you or to be exhaustive in what laws might apply to your particular situation. All that is attempted here, is to give you some sense that laws do exist that could potentially hold your child liable for cyberbullying. In all cases, you need to consult with appropriate counsel and/or your own attorney for proper legal advice.

Chapter 10

LIABILITY OF A PARENT OF A BULLY

Almost every State has some sort of law that holds parents or legal guardians legally responsible for certain conduct of minors.

Usually the laws in the various States make those parents or legal guardians responsible for property damage, personal injury, theft, shoplifting and/or vandalism from the intentional or willful acts of their children.

Most states also have limits on the dollar amount of the liability of parents or legal guardians, and many of the laws have conditions and limits of when liability may be found.

While the laws of each State are different, a quick look at some parental liability law in California is illustrative of the situations in which a parent may be found liable for the conduct of their children:

Intentional Wrongdoing:

"Any act of willful misconduct of a minor that results in injury or death to another person or in any injury to the property of another shall be imputed to the parent or guardian having custody and control of the minor for all purposes of civil damages, and the parent or guardian having custody and control shall be jointly and severally liable with the minor for any damages resulting from the willful misconduct."[72]

Parental liability is limited to $39,300 for each separate tort (or civil wrong) [73]

---

[72] California Civil Code, Section 1714.1(a).

[73] California Civil Code, Section 1714.1(c) and California Rules of Court Appendix B.

> **Intentional Wrongdoing Related to School:**
>
> If a minor willfully causes (1) injury or death to another student, employee or volutneer of private or public school district, and/or (2) real or personal property of school district or employee thereof, then the parent is also liable.
>
> Parental liability here is limited to $18,300 plus any other liability.

So be aware that your State probably has laws that can make you legally responsible for personal injuries or property damage caused by your children to others.

And many States make a parent liable without limit for the conduct of their children, if they knew or should have known the propensity of their child or the actual history of their child as being a bully.

Again, using California as an example of this concept:

> Non Statutory Liability – No Dollar Limit:
>
> Parents on notice (who know or reasonably should know – usually from prior actions) of their child's dangerous propensities are liable for failure to take reasonable efforts to protect others by supervising, restraining and/or correcting the child or warning others of the danger. [74]

But whether or not your State has specific laws that cover cyberbullying, you as a parent could still be sued for and found liable for a host of common law wrongs. The common law of most States can be used to hold a parent liable for the acts of their children, when parents fail to prevent children with

YES
A parent could be sued and found liable for the conduct of their bullying child

---

[74] Robertson v. Wentz (1986) 187 Cal.App.3d 1281; Singer v. Marx (1956) 144 Cal.App.2d 637; Reida v. Lund (1971)18 Cal.App.3d 698; Ellis v. D'Angelo (1953) 116 Cal.App.2d 310; Costello v. Hart (1972) 23 Cal.App.3d 898.

dangerous propensities from committing foreseeable acts and damages.

Some of the non-statutory liability for which a parent could potentially be found liable, include, but are not limited to:

- Assault
- Defamation
- Harassment
- Hate crimes
- Injunctions
- Invasion of privacy
- Intentional Infliction of Emotional Distress
- Negligent Infliction of Emotional Distress
- Negligence and Breach of the Duty of Due Care
- General Negligence
  - Negligent supervision
  - Duty to warn
- Violations of Civil Rights

Liability for these civil wrongs could result in money damages assessed against the parent of the child who bullies for any and all monetary damages suffered by the victim.

Again, please understand that this book is not attempting to provide legal advice to you or to be exhaustive in what laws might apply to your particular situation. All that is attempted here, is to give you some sense that laws do exist that could potentially hold you as a parent liable for the acts of your children. In all cases, you need to consult with appropriate counsel and/or your own attorney for proper legal advice.

Chapter 11

OBLIGATIONS OF A SCHOOL AS TO CYBERBULLYING

Federal Laws

As previously discussed, as of the writing of this book, there are no Federal laws that specifically address cyberbullying.

However, if the type of bullying that takes place is based on race, national origin, color, sex, age, disability or religion, then we are talking about Civil Rights violations for which a number of laws are in place.

Schools are obligated to address conduct that is:

> • "Severe, pervasive or persistent
>
> • Creates a hostile environment at school. That is, it is sufficiently serious that it interferes with or limits a student's ability to participate in or benefit from the services, activities, or opportunities offered by a school
>
> • Based on a student's race, color, national origin, sex disability or religion" [75]

Some of the applicable laws in place for civil rights violations include:

- Title IV and Title VI of the Civil Rights Act of 1964

- Title IX of the Education Amendments of 1972

- Section 504 of the Rehabilitation Act of 1973

---

[75] Source, United States Department of Health & Human Services Stopbullying.gov website.

- Titles II and III of the Americans with Disabilities Act

- Individuals with Disabilities Education Act

As previously discussed, federally funded schools (including primary and secondary schools as well as colleges and universities) have an obligation to resolve harassment problems.

What are those school's obligations for harassment involving protected classes?

The United States Department of Health & Human Services has stated the following:

> "Anyone can report harassing conduct to a school. When a school receives a complaint they must take certain steps to investigate and resolve the situation.
>
> - Immediate and appropriate action to investigate or otherwise determine what happened
>
>   - Inquiry must be prompt, thorough, and impartial
>
>   - Interview targeted students, offending students, and witnesses, and maintain written documentation of investigation
>
> - Communicate with targeted students regarding steps taken to end harassment
>
> - Check in with targeted students to ensure that harassment has ceased
>
> - When an investigation reveals that harassment has occurred, a school should take steps reasonably calculated to:
>   End the harassment
>   Eliminate any hostile environment
>   Prevent harassment from recurring, and
>   Prevent retaliation against the targeted students) or complainant(s)" [76]

---

[76] Source, United States Department of Health & Human Services Stopbullying.gov website.

Suffice it to say for now, that in the event that a school does not resolve the problem, recourse could be had through the U.S. Department of Education's Office for Civil Rights and the U.S. Department of Justice's Civil Rights Division.

Please understand that this book is not attempting to provide legal advice to you or to be exhaustive in what laws might apply to your particular situation. All that is attempted here, is to give you some sense that laws do exist to provide additional protections to you and your children when needed. In all cases, you need to consult with appropriate counsel and/or your own attorney for proper legal advice.

State Laws

Most schools have policies on the use of online and social media when it might affect the school or students or others. Some of those schools even have rules and policies in place that cover bullying and cyberbullying whether the activity is in or out of school.

> What needs to be addressed by parents and schools, is to create a culture of online safety, and digital citizenship by our children

Given the 50 States and thus the 50 sets of laws, it is impractical to provide all of those laws here. Accordingly, you need to look into the laws in your State that set forth the components of your State's anti-bullying laws.

But for the most part, those States that have their own laws related to the obligations of Schools model their laws after the dictates of the Federal laws mentioned above.

Find out what your State laws are as they relate to the obligations of your schools, and be sure to share with your child what they can expect from their schools to help them when a cyberbullying problem exists.

Let your kids know they are not alone in solving a bullying problem, and that not only you, but their school, are there to help.

Chapter 12

WHAT'S A COMMUNITY TO DO TO PREVENT CYBERBULLYING?

If your school or community has not addressed the cyberbullying problem, try to get a cyberbullying prevention program going.

There are amazing resources online and in the library with suggestions on such programs and suggestions for policies and action, but here are just a few[77]:

- Raise awareness of bullying through actions such as surveys of prevalence and role-playing events at assemblies

  - Use anonymous questionnaires for students and educators

- Form a bullying prevention committee which represents the entire school or community and which is responsible for choosing and implementing a prevention program

  - Define bullying and make it clear to the community, all staff and students that bullying of any sort, including cyberbullying, is absolutely unacceptable

  - Adapt and implement bullying prevention policies

---

[77] Source, California Department of Education "*Prevention of Bullying*" webpage: See http://www.cde.ca.gov/ls/ss/se/prevgully.asp.

o   Train all members of the community and school in the appropriate responses to observed incidents of bullying

o   Provide counseling for persistent bullies, targets, and their parents/guardians

o   Regularly review the effectiveness of the anti-bullying program

Everyone needs to actively work towards a community – especially in our schools – that educates our kids on cyberbullying – and makes cyberbullying absolutely unacceptable to all

Chapter 13

WHAT'S A PARENT TO DO TO PREVENT CYBERBULLYING?

Ever Feel This Frustrated With Your Child?

In February 2012, a father posted a video on YouTube showing him shooting his 15-year-old daughter's laptop computer. The father was not happy with Facebook postings by his daughter, and took out that displeasure by killing her laptop! No charges were brought against him after the incident was investigated.

OK, that reaction is a bit excessive, but you have to admit that you've felt like doing the same at some point in time!

In 2013, a father in Grand Prairie, Texas took away a cell phone from his 12-year-old daughter to teach her a lesson for texts he found on her phone. Not an unusual course of conduct for a parent, don't you think? But in this case, the father was arrested and charged with a misdemeanor of theft![78] Here, the daughter was assisted in bringing the criminal charge against her father by her mother, who was separated from the father. The father stood his ground and wanted to fight the charges in court. He was ultimately found not guilty.

It should be noted that the father no longer speaks to his daughter or his ex.

So the caveat here, is that doing the right parental thing for your child does not necessarily mean there won't be strong and hostile emotions involved. Oftentimes doing what is right, is not doing what is easy.

---

[78] Source, The Washington Post.

Some Suggestions On How To Prevent Cyberbullying

Parents and kids can work together to prevent cyberbullying. Some of the suggestions here create the possibility (and in some cases probability) of resistance and a fight by the child.

But isn't a bit of conflict between a parent and child worth it in the long run to keep your children safe?

Some of the ways that a parent and child can work out ways to safely and securely explore technology and the Cyber World, and attempt to prevent cyberbullying include:

- **EDUCATE YOURSELF**

  You can't stop cyberbullying without knowing what it is. You can't protect your kids from the risks of online activity and social media and the Cyber World in general, unless you are an educated parent.

  This book is a starting point for your education, but it is only a starting point. The more you research and talk to friends about their experiences, the more effective you will be as a parent who protects your children.

- **GET TO KNOW THE TECHNOLOGY**

  You might be surprised to know that the Sony PlayStation game consul has a built-in web browser!

  "You can't control what you don't know"

  Actually try out and use your kids' technology and devices so you really know how everything works and what your kids can use the devices to do.

  Stay one step ahead of your kids and take the time to research the various devices your child uses.

Know more than your kids about the devices. Remember, "You can't control what you don't know".

- **CONNECT WITH YOUR KIDS**

Encourage your children to tell you whenever they, or someone they know, is being cyberbullied or is seeing or dealing with uncomfortable online experiences.

Assure your kids that by keeping you informed and letting you know of any problems they are having, that you will not take away their computers or phones or limit or prohibit their access to healthy social media and online content. This fear of losing their technology is one of the principal reasons that kids don't report cyberbullying to adults.

Assure your kids that you won't blame them if they are cyberbullied.

Talk to your kids about online dangers. Communicate honestly and respectfully with them, and be sure to hear them out and let them know that their opinions are important to the process of online safety.

Make sure that what you are trying to build is a partnership with your child of online safety. Merely stating rules without a "buy-in" from your child will be the least effective means of keeping your child safe.

> Be mindful that what parents need to do is create a culture of online safety and responsible citizenship

Make sure that the lines of communication with your child are open at all times. Make sure your kids know that they not only should but they can come to you at any time to discuss any problems they may have in their online and social media world.

- **EDUCATE YOUR KIDS**

Make sure your kids understand all of the issues of cyberbullying. Hopefully this book can help you come up with the type of things to discuss with your kids.

The old saying suggests that "beauty is in the eyes of the beholder". The cyberbullying equivalent is that "bullying is in the mind of the bullied".

What your child thinks is just innocent fun or teasing, might actually be bullying and harassment to another

What this means is that your child needs to be made aware of and made sensitive to the fact that what might be thought of as just innocent fun or teasing of another, might very well be felt by that other person as bullying or harassment.

What should matter to your kids are the feelings and perceptions of others.

- **BE A GOOD EXAMPLE OF HOW TO USE SOCIAL MEDIA AND THE INTERNET**

Model behavior you want your kids to practice. Don't post or tweet while driving.

Don't just click on permissions online or on a cell phone without reading and understanding what you are doing. If you do, it is way too easy to allow another access to your personal and private information.

- **DON'T CONTRIBUTE TO THE PROBLEM**

  Watch out that you don't contribute to the problem of cyberbullying when you use your own social media.

  Posting what you may think are cute pictures of your children on your own web pages or social medial sites, might pose a risk that those pictures or the information you post could be used against your child by cyberbullies.

  Likewise, posting information on your children, including personal information about them, what school they attend, the names of their friends and the like, could prove to be a ripe source of information for cyberbullies to use against your child.

  In fact, consider taking off of your social medial sites any information about and pictures of your child.

- **PROTECT YOUR CHILD'S PASSWORDS**

  Impress upon your child that they should protect their own passwords at all time.

  What this means is that they should keep their passwords and other private information away from prying eyes, and never give out their passwords to anyone without your permission – whether online or live.

  If any of your children's passwords are compromised or thought to be compromised, that password should be immediately replaced.

  Parents should know the passwords for their children's online web sites as well as their social media accounts.

- **LOG OUT OF ONLINE ACCOUNTS**

  No one should save passwords they use online within their browser (either on a computer or on a mobile phone) so that they don't have to enter it the next time they go onto a particular web site. This is especially true when your child uses someone else's computer or mobile phone.

In fact, this is especially true for most kids who walk away from their computer or phone in places that are accessible to others.

While saving passwords online is convenient for the next online access, it poses the significant risk of a subsequent user being able to access your information, as well as a hacker or virus accessing your saved password list and personal information.

Your child should know that they should log out of a password protected site whenever they walk away from or are done using a computer browser or mobile phone, so that no one else can access their private information.

While 90% of youths believe their parents trust them to do what is right online

45% would still change their behavior if they knew their parents were watching

McAfee for Business, 2014 Teens and the Screen study: Exploring Online Privacy, Social Networking and Cyberbullying

- **GAIN ACCESS**

And while we are on the subject of passwords, you should have passwords to your child's devices so that you may have full access at any given moment

Make sure that your child "friends" you online or allows you to "follow" their social media sites so that you can access them whenever you want to see what is going on.

- **CONTROL ACCESS**

  Keep your child's computer in a central location in the house – such as the kitchen or family room. Keep bedrooms technology free.

  If your child's computer is located in a public part of the house and not in the child's bedroom, it is easier to monitor usage.

  In addition, the fact that the computer or mobile phone screen is somewhat public and can be viewed by others while in use, is a self-monitoring influence on your child.

- **LIMIT THE USE OF THE INTERNET AND CELL PHONES**

  As part of controlling access, a parent should also control the amount of time spent online and in cell phone usage.

  Not only is increased time with cyber media the formula for increased possibilities of abuse, but studies have also shown that limiting a child's screen time results in improved sleep, better performance in school, better behavior, and improved overall health[79].

  Just as you would limit TV or computer or gaming systems, so too should you limit cell phone. Especially while driving!

- **GET TO KNOW YOUR CHILD'S ONLINE HABITS**

  Obtain access to all sites and learn who your child's online "friends" are.

---

[79] Iowa State University News Service, March 31, 2014 article entitled, "*Limiting screen time improves sleep, academics and behavior, ISU study finds*".

In fact, know all of the sites visited by your children. Ask them and be sure you know what sites they visit and where they go, what they are doing and who they're doing it with.

In addition, take a look at your child's internet browsing history, and require that the history not be deleted by your child so that you can look at it at any time.

- **KNOW YOUR CHILD'S SCHOOL RULES**

Most schools have policies on the use of online and social media when it might affect the school or students or others. There are a number of schools that have rules and policies in place that cover bullying and cyberbullying whether the activity is in or out of school.

An overview of some typical school obligations relating to setting out rules are provided in Chapter 11.

Find out from the school if these sorts of polices are in place, and make sure you know the rules and that your child knows those rules as well.

- **SET YOUR OWN GROUND RULES**

Set rules and limits of use as well as consequences for failure to abide by rules. Parents can even find sample guidelines as well as instructions for setting privacy settings at web sites such as Family Online Safety Institute[80].

Make sure your kids are aware of and smart about what they post or say. Your kids need to be aware and cautious about who they let see their information and pictures. Educate your children on how people who aren't actual friends can use the information and pictures that are posted and made public.

---

[80] See www.fosi.org.

- **GET SOCIAL**

  Stay knowledgeable about the newest and latest social networks

  Understand how the accounts work if your kids are on them.

  Create your own "profile" and "friend" your child

- **USE FILTERING AND MONITORING SOFTWARE AND MOBILE APPLICATIONS[81]**

  Some software suites like Norton and McAfee, allow you to monitor your child's usage and control access to web sites and social media.

  Web and social media site monitoring can be done with various software and mobile apps. A mere few of the many available software and mobile apps worth looking at are:

  - **CellSafety (Mobile App)**
  - **Cyber Patrol Online Protection (Software)**
  - **eBlaster Mobile for Android (Mobile App)**
  - **GoGoStat's Parental Guidance (Mobile App)**
  - **iHound Mobile Phone and Family Tracker (Mobile App)**
  - **Kids Place – Parental Control (Mobile App)**
  - **KidsWatch (Software)**
  - **McAfee (Software)**
  - **Mobicip (Mobile App)**
  - **My Mobile Watchdog (Mobile and Web App)**
  - **Norton (Software)**
  - **Net Nanny (Mobile App and Software)**

---

[81] The author and publisher have no financial interest in any software or application mentioned in this book. The listing of any software or application is not meant to be exhaustive and is provided for representative, and hopefully helpful purposes only. The author and publisher make no recommendation of any software or application for use by anyone – that decision is left solely to the reader.

- **PureSight PC (Software and Mobile App)**
- **Safe Brower Parental Control (Mobile App)**
- **Safe Eyes Mobile (Mobile App)**
- **SafetyWeb (Software)**
- **SocialShield (Software)**
- **SpectorSoft (Software)**
- **TeenSafe (Mobile App)**
- **Trend Micro's Online Guardian for Families (Software)**
- **uKnowKids (Software and Mobile App)**
- **YouDiligence (Software)**
- **WebWatcher (Software and Mobile App)**

- **SET PRIVACY SETTINGS**

  These should be checked regularly in the settings of the browser being used and with regard to each web site and social media site being accessed.

  - **REPUTATION MANAGEMENT**

  What goes online

  Stays online

  Make sure your kids are aware that anything they post online does not have an expiration date.

  Let your kids know about a "digital footprint" and the permanency of online activity. Let them know that anything posted online can come back to haunt your kids when applying for college or for jobs.

  It should always be remembered that "WHAT GOES ONLINE STAYS ONLINE"!

- ## "GOOGLE" YOURSELF AND YOUR CHILD AND SEE IF THERE ARE ALREADY ANY PROBLEMS

  Everyone should periodically do an online search through a search engine such as Google, to see if there are any problems already online that compromise privacy or reputation or that could be used by cyberbullies.

  By doing so, your child and you can then do whatever is possible to correct or remove the information before it could pose any problem for your child.

- ## PAUSE BEFORE POSTING OR HITTING "SEND"

  Just the mere practice of pausing and re-reading and thinking about a posting or message before sending it off into the Cyber World gives time to reflect on whether that posting or message can come back to harm your child.

  An unthought out or hastily sent posting or message could not only be used against your child by a bully, but it could also affect future opportunities for school admissions and getting a job.

- ## CONTROL YOUR TONE

  Your child should be reminded that the more polite and respectful he or she is online, the less likely there will be a hostile and bullying response.

  Our kids need to recognize that reading a text message or email or online posting cannot always convey the tone that would be apparent when speaking face-to-face. As a result, it is too easy for the recipient of the message to misinterpret the tone of the message. Your child needs to be careful with every message sent.

  And of course, sending messages when angry or overly emotional can cause additional problems.

- **REGULARLY REVIEW TEXT AND INSTANT MESSAGING**

  Regularly review your child's instant messages. Review who is on their "Buddy List" and make sure you know who those people are and how your child knows those people.

  Since our kids oftentimes use acronyms in many of their texts and messaging, get to know what they are and what they mean. Ask your kids whenever you see an acronym what it means.

  If you take a look at the Appendix, you can see a short list of common acronyms that every Parent should be aware of. But rest assured there are a lot more, and a lot more new ones are coming.

- **REGULARLY MONITOR EMAIL**

  Regularly review your child's email. Oftentimes you can find email that your child deleted, still in the Trash folder of the email account.

  Again, be mindful of the acronyms and know what your kids are actually saying!

- **DON'T OPEN UNIDENTIFIED OR UNSOLICITED MESSAGES**

  Any sort of message – emails, texts, Facebook messages, etc. – that is from someone your child or you don't know, should not be opened.

  Not only could such messages be from bullies, but they also may contain offensive content, or viruses or improper links.

- **DON'T OPEN ATTACHMENTS FROM UNIDENTIFIED OR UNKNOWN PEOPLE**

   Attachments from unidentified people or from unsolicited or unknown sources, can at worst contain viruses designed to collect private information. At best, they could take your child to improper or offensive online content.

- **MONITOR THE PICTURES YOUR CHILD POSTS**

   It's probably impossible or unrealistic to expect your child to never post a picture (especially of him or herself) online. But it is not impossible or unrealistic for a parent to know what and where pictures are being posted before your child posts.

   Kids should know that all photos (or anything for that matter) that is posted online, is subject to everyone seeing it – including parents, grandparents and the like. In addition, photos and information posted online could also be used by bullies against your child.

- **KEEP YOUR KIDS AWAY FROM QUESTIONNAIRES, FREE GIVEAWAYS AND CONTESTS**

   Many of these ruses are to obtain personal information from your kids. Kids should just not participate in anything of the sort without Parents' involvement and only on a known safe website.

- **NO UNDERAGE FACEBOOK**

   Facebook requires its users to be 13 years of age or older. You should not allow Facebook use until 13 AND only if you are comfortable with your child using Facebook.

At least 38% of kids on Facebook are under the age of 13[82]! Your child should not be one of them.

- ## FIRST STEPS IF CYBERBULLYING HAPPENS

First off, don't ignore the cyberbullying thinking that the kids are able to work it all out without adult help. Intervene immediately as necessary, and of course, get other adults to help when necessary.

Make sure everyone is safe and meet any immediate medical or mental health needs.

Stay calm and reassure the kids involved, including bystanders.

- ## DON'T DELETE THE CYBERBULLYING

Definitely don't delete the cyberbullying! You may need it as proof at some point, so keep the evidence.

Be sure to save the URLs of the location where the cyberbullying took place. Document the evidence such as printing out emails or webpages. Take screen shots of the cyberbullying where possible.

- ## DON'T RESPOND TO CYBERBULLYING

Don't allow your child to escalate the problem by responding or trying to "get back".

Also, the bully may actually hope for some sort of response – and the response itself might be fodder for further cyberbullying.

---

[82] ZDNet, April 13, 2012

- **DON'T RETALIATE**

  All this will do is turn your child into a bully and escalate
  the problem.

- **BLOCK THE BULLY**

  Use program or app preferences or settings or privacy tools
  to completely block the bully.

  If a bully is in a chat room with your child your child
  should immediately leave the chat room.

  Your child or you could delete the bully from email
  contacts and social networks and even from a phone.
  Instant messaging could be blocked.

  There is no reason your child needs to receive and be
  subject to any more online cyberbullying.

- **CHANGE ACCOUNT SETTINGS**

  If things really get bad and the cyberbullying can't be
  stopped for any reason, you could help your child change
  account settings or close down existing accounts and open
  new and more protected accounts.

  Screen names and passwords could be changed, profile
  pictures could be deleted, remove access to your child's
  social media by anyone other than confirmed friends and
  family.

- **REPORT THE CYBERBULLY**

  Depending upon the social media or online site being used
  or accessed, there is usually a mechanism provided to
  report a cyberbully to the administrator of the site.

  A report should be done immediately, with copies of the
  proof obtained (screen shots, etc.) sent to support the need

for the administrator of the site to take action against the bully.

Your child should report the cyberbullying to you, or a teacher in school, or any other responsible adult for further handling.

A report can be made to online and mobile phone service providers. Bullying would violate terms of service by a provider and the bully could be penalized by the service provider itself.

Your child should know that he or she is not alone, and that not only will the social media sites themselves provide assistance, but so will the adults in his or her life.

- **GET THE SCHOOL INVOLVED**

As previously mentioned, most schools have policies on the use of online and social media when it might affect the school or students or others. Some of those schools even have rules and policies in place that cover bullying and cyberbullying whether the activity is in or out of school.

An overview of some typical school obligations relating to setting out rules are provided in Chapter 11. What you will find, is that most schools are going to have to do something about the cyberbullying.

So again, you should find out from the school if these sorts of polices are in place. Make sure you know the rules and that your child knows those rules as well.

- **GET LAW ENFORCEMENT INVOLVED**

If need be, law enforcement could be called when the level of bullying rises to that of a crime.

More detail on the various type of criminal issues related to cyberbullying have been discussed earlier in this book.

- **IF NEED BE, SUE**

  If need be, you might have to get the Courts involved to stop any further cyberbullying. You would want to see an attorney to find out your rights and what remedies are available to you, including getting an injunction or restraining order.

  If there are legitimate damages and costs incurred as a result of the cyberbullying, you may also want to sue for appropriate damages to hold the cyberbully responsible.

  And if the bully doesn't stop, then an injunction to stop future bullying might also be appropriate and available to you and your child.

- **DON'T BE SO QUICK**
  TO TAKE THE TECHNOLOGY AWAY

  REMEMBER! Your child derives their social outlet, for the most part, online. So, don't be so quick to take their technology away without some real thought.

  This is tantamount to taking away their social world! It is easily felt as a form of punishment when you think you are trying to protect your child.

REMEMBER

Cutting off your child's technology is tantamount to cutting off your child's social world

And

Communicates to your child your lack of trust

**IN PROTECTING YOUR CHILDREN
DON'T FORGET
THE PARENTAL LOVE
AND UNDERSTANDING
NECESSARY IN EVERYTHING
THAT YOU DO**

**GOOD LUCK AND
KEEP YOUR KIDS SAFE!**

Appendix

SOME INTERNET ACRONYMS EVERY PARENT SHOULD KNOW

After you read this list, you'll likely start looking at your child's texts in a whole new way!

1174	Party meeting place – nude club
1337	Elite –or- leet –or- 1337
143, 459 or ILU	I love you
182	I hate you
420	Marijuana
53X	Sex
8	Oral sex
9	Parent watching
99	Parent gone
ADR	Address
AEAP	As early as possible
ALAP	As late as possible
AMEZRU	I am easy, are you?
ASL	Age/sex/location
BRB	Be right back
Broken	Hungover from alcohol
CD9	Parents around/code 9
CID	Acid (the drug)

C-P	Sleepy
CTN	Can't talk now
CU46	See you for sex
CWYL	Chat with you later
CYT	See you tomorrow
DOC	Drug of choice
F2F	Face to face. Asking for a meeting or video chat
GNOC	Get naked on camera
GYPO	Get your pants off
HAK	Hugs and kisses
IMHO	In my humble opinion
IMNSHO	In my not so humble opinion
IPN	I'm posting naked
IWSN	I want sex now
J/K	Jerking off
KFY or K4Y	Kiss for you
KOTL	Kiss on the lips
KPC	Keeping parents clueless
L8R	Later
LH6	Let's have sex
LMIRL	Let's meet in real life
LMK	Let me know
LOL	Laughing out loud
MOOS	Member of the opposite sex

MORF or RUMORF	Male or female, or are your male or female?
MOS	Mom over shoulder
MOSS	Member of the same sex
MPFB	My personal fuck buddy
NALOPKT	Not a lot of people know that
NAZ	Name/address/zip
NIFOC	Naked in front of computer
NM	Never mind
NMU	Not much, you?
nOOb	Newbie or someone inexperienced
P911	Parent alert
PAL	Parents are listening
PAW	Parents are watching
PIR	Parent in room
POS	Parent over shoulder
PRON	Porn
Q2C	Quick to cum
ROFLMAO	Rolling on the floor laughing my ass off
ROTFL	Rolling on the floor laughing
RU/18	Are you over 18?
RUH	Are you horny?
RUMORF	Are you male or female?
S2R	Send to receive
SOHF	Sense of humor failure

SORG	Straight or gay
SUGARPIC	Suggestive or erotic photo
TDTM	Talk dirty to me
THOT	That hoe over there
TWD	Texting while driving
WTF	What the fuck
WTTP	Want to trade pictures?
WUF	Where you from?
WYCM	Will you call me?
WYRN	What's your real name?
ZERG	To gang up on someone